On Your Confirmation

Selected by
Peter Dainty

**kevin
mayhew**

Heavenly Father, I realise that you have loved me
    and been present with me
    since before I was born.
Now I shall acknowledge your love
    in the presence of your people.
Give me your Holy Spirit
    so that I may respond with my own love for you,
    all the days of my life.

Peter Dainty

Lord Jesus Christ,
   I thank you for all the benefits
   you have won for me,
   for all the pains and insults
   you have borne for me.

Most merciful redeemer,
   friend and brother,
   may I know you more clearly,
   love you more dearly,
   and follow you more nearly,
   day by day.
Amen.

Richard of Chichester (c.1197-c.1253)

Jesus –
through the bread
and the wine
of Communion,
I am in you
and you are in me.

It's a holy mystery
how a small piece of bread
and a sip of wine
can fill me with your presence.

You are the Bread of Heaven;
bread of the world too.
May my own life
nourish and feed
those who are in need.
Amen.

Susan Hardwick

Spirit of Jesus,
   wind, water, fire, come.
Spirit of Jesus,
   God's anointing, come.
Spirit of Jesus
   my strengthener, come.
Spirit of Jesus,
   loving heart of God, come.
Spirit of Jesus,
   dove of divine peace, come.
Spirit of Jesus,
   foretaste of the glory of God, come.
Spirit of Jesus,
   creative breath stronger than death, come.
Come, Holy Spirit,
   my friend and my life.

Lord, make me an instrument
  of your peace.
Where there is hatred,
  let me sow love;
  where there is injury,
  pardon;
  where there is discord,
  union;
  where there is doubt,
  faith;
  where there is despair,
  hope;
  where there is darkness,
  light;
  where there is sadness,
  joy.

Attributed to St Francis

Lord Jesus,
   I give you my hands
      to do your work.
   I give you my feet
      to go your way.
   I give you my eyes
      to see as you do.
   I give you my tongue
      to speak your words.
   I give you my mind,
      that you may think in me.

I give you my spirit,
   that you may pray in me.
Above all
   I give you my heart,
      that you may love through me.

I give you my whole self,
   that you may grow in me,
   so that it is you, Lord Jesus,
   who live and work and love
   in me.

The Grail Prayer

Jesus,
  now I belong to you!
Take my life,
  all that I am
  and hope to be,
  and use it to your glory.

May the promises
  I made at my Confirmation
  be lived out
  in my life.

May the joy of that day
   run like a golden river
   through all my days.

May my life be
   a jam-packed yell of praise,
   a roller-coaster ride
   of celebration
   that you have called me
   to follow you.
Amen.

Susan Hardwick

Jesus, I don't understand me at all –
    and nor does anyone else
    it often seems.

But you do.

In all this confusing time
    of growing up,
    stay close by.
Guide me.
Keep me safe.
Amen.

Susan Hardwick

Jesus, you know me
  through and through.
It's no use pretending
  with you.

With you, I can say it
  – or shout or scream it! –
  just the way it really is;
  just the way I really feel.
Thank you!
Amen.

Susan Hardwick

Dear God,
  my heavenly parent,
    forgive me.
  I'm so sorry
    for what I said and did.
  Please forgive me.
  Help me
    not to do it again.
Amen.

Susan Hardwick

Dear God,
  thank you
    for forgiving me!
  thank you
    for the sense
    of peace
    and of wholeness
    your forgiveness brings!
Amen.

Susan Hardwick

Jesus,
  it's really hard and lonely sometimes
  walking the Christ-path, isn't it?
And especially when people name-call
  and jeer at what you believe.

They don't understand
  about you, Lord,
  and all that you've done –
  for them
  as well as for me.

Give me the words
  with which to answer them.

Make me a courageous witness
  to your love and your truth.

Help me find
  other young people
  to travel the Christ-path
  with me.
Amen.

Susan Hardwick

Jesus,
  you are my constant
  and faithful
  and loving friend.

  Any time,
  any place,
  wherever I am,
  whatever my need,
  I know you hear me;
  I know you are near me;
  I thank you and praise you!
Amen.

Susan Hardwick

Jesus,
  I offer today,
  with whatever it may bring,
  as a gift to you.

  Take it and bless it.

  Walk through it with me.

  May all I say, and all I do,
  be worthy of you.
Amen.

Susan Hardwick

Jesus,
   as you hung on your cross,
   you prayed
   that those who had so hurt you
   would be forgiven.

I'm hurting, too,
   both inside and out,
   from what was done to me.

Help me to forgive them.
Help me to let go
   of the anger I feel.

Susan Hardwick

Dear Jesus,
   thank you
   for helping me to forgive.

Thank you
   for setting me free
   from the darkness
   of that bitterness and hurt.

Thank you
   for making
   the sun shine again.
Amen.

Susan Hardwick

When the going gets tough,
it's tempting to give in
and to give up.
That's when I need you,
Jesus,
more than ever.
Stay very close by.
Give me stickability.
Keep me faithful
to what I have to do,
just as you were.
Amen.

Susan Hardwick

Father,
 it's hard sometimes to know,
 amongst all the amazing possibilities,
 the confusing and tempting
 choices and voices,
 how to keep my balance;
 to know what's right for me.
 ,So hold me steady and true.
  May I keep my eyes
  fixed always on you.
Amen.

Susan Hardwick

Dear God –
  you know
  what I want.
You also know
  what I need!
So –
  I'll just leave it
  up to you to decide
  what's best.
You're more likely
  to get it right
  than me.
Amen.

Susan Hardwick

God –
   life is really hard
   just at present.
Be a light for me
   in the dark,
   a strong hand to hold.
Amen.

Susan Hardwick

There's such a mystery
  about you, Lord.
The more I find out,
  the less I seem really to know!
Learning about you
  is a never-ending
  voyage of discovery.

And yet —
  you are far, far closer to me
  than I am to myself.

You are
    my most intimate companion.
You love me
    from the inside out.

Help me
    to see you everywhere.
Help me
    to know you in everyone.
Help my understanding.
Amen.

Susan Hardwick

Dear God,
  once I used to think
  it'd be nice to know the future.

But now I see
  that it's not such a great idea,
  after all!
If I could predict it,
  then I'd be tempted
  to find my own ways
  of getting through,
  rather than trusting it to you
  to plan the best route.

,So -
  Creator
  and Lord of life,
   and of this fantastic world,
  I place my future
  - with all its possibilities
  and all its promise -
  into your hands.
You know the way.
Keep me sensitive
  to your will for me.
Make the road straight.
Keep my footsteps true.
May my whole life
  be a close dance with you.
Amen.

Susan Hardwick

27

O Jesus, I have promised
   to serve you to the end.
Lord, be for ever near me,
   my Master and my Friend.
I shall not fear the battle,
   if you are by my side,
nor wander from the pathway
   if you will be my Guide.

John Ernest Bode (1816-74)

God be in my head
   and in my understanding.
God be in my eyes
   and in my looking.
God be in my mouth
   and in my speaking.
God be in my heart
   and in my thinking.
God be at my end
   and at my departing.

Book of Hours (1514)

Lord, at this important time in my life,
  I trust the past to your mercy,
  the present to your love,
  and the future to your guidance.

Now may the grace of our Lord Jesus Christ,
   the love of God our Father,
   and the companionship of the Holy Spirit
   be with us all,
   for evermore.
Amen.

First published in 2004 by

KEVIN MAYHEW LTD
Buxhall, Stowmarket, Suffolk, IP14 3BW
E-mail: info@kevinmayhewltd.com

9 8 7 6 5 4 3 2 1

ISBN 1 84417 349 6
Catalogue No. 1500761

Designed by Angela Selfe
Illustrations by Angela Palfrey

Printed and bound in China